How to be a Good Farmer

by Liz Miles

Illustrated by Anjan Sarkar

OXFORD

UNIVERSITY PRESS

Gail rears sheep and cows.

Abad rears goats.

Hana is a flower farmer.

Gail

In summer, I get the sheep down from the hills.

<u>Perhaps</u> the dog will help Gail get the sheep.
Do you think the dog will help or won't help?

The sheep dog prowls near the sheep until they are in the barn!

I shear the sheep in the summer.
They feel secure in this barn.

Keeping the sheep secure makes them feel <u>calm</u>.
What makes you feel <u>calm</u>?

I must look for a pair of lost sheep.
Never fear! They will turn up.

Abad

It is hot! I must <u>check</u> that my goats are well.

How could Abad <u>check</u> that his goats are okay?

8

The soil is not moist. The crops might fail. The goats must look harder for food.

There is a <u>chance</u> that the crops will not grow. Does that mean they might not grow or that they definitely will not grow?

My goats are good at looking for food!

Now they are looking for food higher up!

Look!

Can you say the word 'look' to show that Abad <u>exclaims</u> it? Should you say it in a quiet whisper or a loud, excited voice?

Hana

For much of the year, my farm has lots of flowers.

In summer, I ensure the flowers are kept moist.

The farmer's helper is walking <u>between</u> the rows of flowers. Can you walk <u>between</u> two things?

The sooner the flowers get to the shops, the better.

We are all good farmers!

Think About the Book

Can you match the animal or crop to the right farmer?